"Unraveling Words: Navigating Dyslexia's Labyrinth":

By

NEVILLE LAWSON

TABLE OF CONTENTS

INTRODUCTION

In a society that embraces and encourages diversity, every individual has unique competencies, capabilities, and issues. Dyslexia is one such trouble that has fascinated and confounded lecturers and educators for the long term. This international mastering hole impacts hundreds of thousands of people and has an enormous effect on how they live and examine the sector. Despite this, stigma and misinformation about dyslexia are common.

We kindly encourage you to go searching." Unlocking the Power of Dyslexia: A Roadmap to Success
In this book, we move substantially into the problem of dyslexia and reveal the numerous viewpoints of individuals who address it each day. It is an exploration of knowledge and empowerment.

The motive of this guide is to clarify dyslexia and refute popular myths. It is a blend of in-depth studies and honest adoration for the tenacity of the human soul. We agree that by highlighting the subtleties of dyslexia, we will encourage greater expertise and support for individuals who are bothered by this anguish. Knowledge, in our opinion, is the premise for advancement.

We will walk hand in hand via these pages as we take an excursion through the history of dyslexia, following its beginnings from the earliest documented observations to the modern-day expertise produced through modern research. By investigating the neurological underpinnings and cognitive characteristics of dyslexia, we hope to offer readers a higher expertise of how it operates.

This manual, however, goes a lot beyond a scholarly enterprise. We need to attract interest in the daily demanding situations and triumphs faced by way of dyslexic humans. Through their private studies, we're going to discover the profound effects dyslexia has had on shaping the identities of several human beings, such as students, specialists, artists, and leaders.

We understand that dyslexia no longer takes place in a vacuum, that's the most critical component. Families, educators, and communities may also assist human beings with dyslexia to attain their complete ability with the aid of using the beneficial hints and assets in this booklet. By cooperating and displaying compassion, we can build a lifestyle that values the contributions of people with dyslexia and recognizes their competencies.

We also look at the rapidly developing vicinity of generation and innovation where assistive gadgets and inclusive practices are converting the educational and professional panorama for dyslexic human beings. By persevering to live at the cutting edge of increase, we try to stop all of us from falling back off because of gaining knowledge of demanding situations.

We ask you to reflect on your information about dyslexia as we read through these pages collectively and put off any lingering myths. Whether you're a dyslexic seeking out support and notions or a best friend dedicated to setting up an extra-inclusive workplace, this manual intends to provide you with the expertise, empathy, and assets you need to make a big exchange.

I think that every dyslexic character may reach their full capacity if dyslexia is better understood, the form of human intelligence is common, and supportive surroundings are created. Regardless of the ways their minds recognize the written language, permits set out in this direction to create a global in which all people live blissfully and are preferred for their specific capabilities.

Chapter 1

"Unlocking the World of Dyslexia"

In the sizable geography of human variability, dyslexia is a unique and captivating trait that affects how people perceive and utilize language. Despite ordinary or above-common intelligence and the right coaching opportunities, dyslexics battle with analyzing, spelling, and writing. An identifiable mastering incapacity is dyslexia. We observe the definition, records, kinds, and characteristics of dyslexia in this introductory bankruptcy to help readers recognize the challenging surroundings that dyslexic persons should navigate.

The Evolution of Dyslexia

The word dyslexia was first used in the late nineteenth century by way of German ophthalmologist Rudolf Berlin. The word is an aggregate of the Greek words;dys; (trouble) and & lexia; (phrases or language). Over time, lots have advanced in our understanding of dyslexia. We now are aware of it to be a neurological condition delivered by utilizing the intricate wiring of the brain. Due to the numerous methods by which humans with dyslexia process language, they have trouble deciphering phrases, recognizing letters, and organizing written fabric.

Dyslexia's Development

There is an extended record of misdiagnosis, demonization, and false impression of dyslexia. Early misconceptions related dyslexia to indifference, foolishness, or imaginative and prescient issues. It wasn't until the latter half of the 20th century that researchers, teachers, and advocates started to fully realize the nature of dyslexia. The groundbreaking paintings of people like Dr. Samuel Orton and Anna Gillingham allowed for the advent of specific teaching methods for dyslexic youngsters.

Many kinds and signs of dyslexia

Dyslexia can happen in a whole lot of approaches, and everybody may have a unique revel in it. There is no one-size-fits-all profile, although there are positive commonplace characteristics.
-Struggles to recognize phrases fluently and precise

-Problems psychologically separating terms into their man or woman sounds

-Grammar and writing mistakes

-Studying comprehension is hard, regardless of speaking the language

-Difficulties with organization, time control, and sequencing

Bear in mind that dyslexia doesn't necessarily mean Loss of intelligence or cognitive potential.

-There are precise abilities that dyslexics can possess oftentimes, they are creativity, fixing problems, and unusual questioning.

Detection and prevalence

People of numerous a long time, social conditions, and linguistic backgrounds can experience dyslexia, which is a not-unusual sickness. It affects millions of people globally. However, it is believed that five–10% of human beings may be dyslexic. Prevalence rates range depending on the diagnostic criteria used.

It is difficult to determine if a person has dyslexia and includes massive trying out, along with opinions on their cognitive and educational potential, assessments of their academic accomplishment, and an analysis of their strengths and weaknesses. Effective therapy that can appreciably affect a dyslexic person's instructional profession and well-being ought to be provided as soon as possible after the condition is identified.

As we begin our adventure toward better expertise of dyslexia, permit me to lay apart our assumptions and rejoice in the brilliance of dyslexic minds. The chapters that follow will talk about the neurological underpinnings of dyslexia, sensible assist and intervention techniques, and inspirational memories of dyslexic human beings who have triumphed over barriers to gain greatness. If we arm ourselves with understanding and empathy, we can create a tradition that now not only accepts but also values the particular characteristics of individuals with dyslexia.

Chapter 2

"Decoding the Dyslexic Brain: A Journey into the Neurological Differences

The dyslexic brain's inner workings are fascinatingly shown in this chapter. We explore the neurological underpinnings of dyslexia, shedding light on the intricate mechanisms affecting how language is perceived and processed by dyslexic people. For dyslexic learners to receive successful therapy and be in an environment that supports them, it is essential to comprehend these neurological anomalies.

Anatomy and Function of the Dyslexic Brain

Our thoughts, feelings, and behaviors are controlled by an intricate and interconnected network of neurons in the human brain. Dyslexics' brains may be structurally and functionally different from non-dyslexics in certain regions that are crucial for reading and language processing. Modern neuroimaging methods, including functional magnetic resonance imaging (fMRI) and diffusion tensor imaging (DTI), have been crucial in understanding these variances.

The posterior parts of the left hemisphere of the brain, which include the parietotemporal and occipitotemporal areas, have drawn a lot of attention in research. The ability to recognize words visually and phonological processing—the ability to recognize and alter spoken sounds—both depend on these regions. In dyslexic people, these regions may have atypical activation patterns, which might affect reading and language-related abilities.

both environmental and genetic influences

The prevalence of dyslexia in families and the availability of specific genetic markers linked to reading difficulties both point to a significant hereditary component of the disorder. The genetics of dyslexia are complex and multifaceted, involving the interaction of numerous genes and environmental factors. Several candidate genes have been identified as potentially contributing to dyslexia.

The environment can influence how dyslexic people improve their reading abilities in a variety of ways, including early language exposure, instructional strategies, and resource accessibility. Reading competence can be promoted and dyslexia's negative effects can be lessened with early intervention and great teaching strategies tailored to each student's needs.

Cognitive and Neurological Mechanisms

The cognitive activity of reading has several facets and calls for a variety of interrelated abilities. The following cognitive processes are affected by dyslexia:

-The tendency to comprehend and phantom the effects of certain sounds in spoken words.

It's hard for dyslexics to understand and encode languages because they battle with phonemic interest.

- **Rapid Automatic Naming (RAN):** The capability of quickly naming detected visual symbols, such as letters or numbers. Poor RAN skills are associated with reading difficulties in dyslexia.

- **Working Memory**: The ability to briefly save and use statistics. Working reminiscence troubles in dyslexics may make it extra hard for them to not forget and method information whilst analyzing.

Dyslexia is a complex condition that involves more than just phonological difficulties. Dyslexia can affect how dyslexics see and recognize written material, as well as visual processing problems.

Understanding the tricky interactions between those cognitive functions and their neurological bases offers critical insights into how humans with dyslexia see the worlds of studying and language.

We discover a panorama of tremendous intricacy and areas of expertise as we discover deeper into the brain causes of dyslexia. This know-how places us in a better function to provide a focused remedy, make the maximum of our strengths, and foster inclusive surroundings that value the form of dyslexic minds. We will look at practical techniques for early detection, intervention, and supportive education within the following chapters to assist dyslexic adolescents in achieving their instructional and extracurricular efforts.

Chapter 3

Intervention and early detection.

"Nurturing Potential: The Power of Early Support for Dyslexic Learners"

In this instance, the emphasis is on how crucially important early identification and intervention are for dyslexic people. Parents, teachers, and caregivers must first recognize dyslexia in its early stages to focus assistance and lay the foundation for academic success and psychological growth. We can help create an environment that dyslexic learners can achieve by understanding the signs of dyslexia and implementing evidence-based interventions.

Finding children with dyslexia early

Dyslexia typically manifests early, while children are still learning to read and write. Although it can be challenging to identify dyslexia in young children because some of the difficulties may be mistaken for normal developmental stages, dyslexia is a learning disability. Therefore, it's important to be alert for the following early warning signs:

- Problems with language – Blending, segmentation, and rhyming failure –

Spelling or adding letters to sound problems.

- Inconsistent letter names or memory loss

- The problem of understanding which sentences are perpetual.

-Mixing of letters "b" and "d", rear or mirrored display; Dot avoidance and writing aversion.

Knowing those indicators can assist parents, educators, and others proactively searching for expert evaluation and help, making sure that dyslexic kids acquire spark-off intervention.

Assessment and screening should be done early.

Early dyslexia screening is necessary to identify at-risk children and provide the necessary care before reading difficulties deteriorate. Standardized tests, chance encounters, and parent-teacher questionnaires are just a few of the assessment tools that could aid in early detection. Together, parents, educators, and healthcare professionals must have a full grasp of a child's strengths and shortcomings.

The child's phonological awareness, reading fluency, spelling, and other reading and language-related cognitive processes can be further examined with tests designed particularly for dyslexia after the condition has been identified.

These tests support the identification of dyslexia and help tailor interventions to target specific issue areas.

Methods for Effective Early Intervention

The first step in assisting dyslexic youngsters and preventing academic failure is early intervention which has shown that complete, organized, and methodical interventions are the most effective for improving reading skills. The following approaches and strategies are only a few of those backed by data.

-Multisensory Structured Language Instruction: The use of several sensory modalities such as audio, visual, and kinesthetic assists students in learning and gaining phonological awareness, decoding, and orthography abilities more effectively.

- **Phonics guidance**: This strategy teaches children from an early stage that letters and sounds combine to create the words of decoding exceptional sentences.

- **Common Sight terms**: Hard words can be found everywhere in these texts.

- Practice reading fluently to improve the reading fluency of your study.

- Creating Environmental Factors That Promote Empathy, Autonomy, and Growth in Dyslexic college students.

Early intervention, which improves reading competencies at the same time as additionally improving shallowness and force, lays the basis for ongoing instructional fulfillment.

The functions of parents and teachers

Parents and educators play an important role in the method of early detection and intervention. If households and schools collaborate to install robust partnerships, dyslexic college students can benefit from ongoing awareness and help. By being open and sincere about the child's development and demanding situations, dads, moms, and teachers can collaborate to lay out tailor-made studying plans that don't forget every baby's precise competencies and goals.

Supporting an environment that is dyslexia-friendly in colleges and groups additionally promotes inclusivity and expertise. In an assessment of the mother and father, who can discover resources and networks to support them along the way, educators can gain expert improvement with the aid of gaining knowledge about dyslexia and efficient coaching methods.

By embracing the potential of early identification and intervention, we provide dyslexic kids the opportunity to embark on a path of discovery and growth. We look at the impact of dyslexia on learning and development in Chapter 4. As dyslexic students advance through their school careers, we also examine strategies for supporting their resilience and sense of value.

Chapter 4:

The Impact of Dyslexia on Learning and Development

"Releasing Potential: Exploring Instructive Challenges Because of Dyslexia"

Let us investigate the enormous influence dyslexia has on learning and development, including cognitive, emotional, and social components. Knowing the problems that dyslexic kids confront enables us to provide focused interventions that build resilience, self-esteem, and a positive academic experience.

Dyslexic students have educational challenges.

Dyslexia has a profound impact on learning, especially in areas such as reading, writing, and spelling. Dyslexic students frequently face the following challenges:

Reading problems: Problems of accurate and fluent word recognition leading to slow reading and poor understanding.

Spelling Hardships: Division and articulation of sounds in words prompting incorrect spellings.

- **Difficulties with Creating**: Befuddled considerations that can frustrate the technique engaged with forming.

- **Data Handling**: Dyslexic students could struggle with gaining from direct talks as they will more often than not consume most of the day to procure and coordinate such data from guidelines.

- **Testing and Appraisal**: Execution on normalized tests may be restricted on account of a dyslexic understudy as they could have perusing and composing weaknesses that are not represented.

Emotional and Social Implications

Dyslexic students may experience substantial emotional and social consequences as a result of the academic difficulty connected with dyslexia. Academic challenges and peer comparisons can result in feelings of anger, shame, and inadequacy. People who are dyslexic may acquire negative attitudes toward learning, which can lead to disengagement and decreased motivation.

Moreover, dyslexic kids can be socially distraught by names, for example, "slow", or "languid" which are credited due to their concerns with perusing and composing. These issues incorporate harassment, prompting confidence challenges that block their general prosperity.

Increasing Self-Esteem and Resilience

To flourish in their scholastics and individual lives, dyslexic understudies need to construct strength and confidence as they face difficulties. Here are a few systems for building flexibility and confidence:

- **Self-Advocacy Skills:** Encourage dyslexic students to express their needs and seek assistance when needed. Self-advocacy education helps students manage their educational journey more effectively.

Emphasize that people can develop their talents with effort and commitment. Do not conceal your mistakes; mistakes are a part of life and learning.

- Lay out an engaging environment with straightforwardness and affirmation of different learning styles.

To give cooperative assistance, guardians and teachers should cooperate.

Collaboration among parents, educators, and other support providers is critical in the development of dyslexic students. There should be routes for exchanging information regarding a student's success, problems, and special needs. Working together, parents and educators can create personalized learning plans, revise them as needed, and give focused interventions to help their child's academic growth.

Educators can use dyslexia-friendly teaching strategies such as allocating more time for reading and writing tasks, using audiobooks, and incorporating assistive technology. Individualized Education Plans (IEPs) and 504 Plans can specify particular adjustments and supports for dyslexic pupils.

Accepting Diversity and Promoting Inclusion

Parents and instructors have to cooperate to help.

It is important to raise dyslexia awareness and nurture a supportive culture, in turn providing a conducive environment for all students' success. Teachers and other school staff can be trained on dyslexia; this will give them information and competencies to handle students who suffer from dyslexia in schools.

By recognizing dyslexics' strengths and potential, we may make learning more fun for them. We will look at how assistive technology can help dyslexic pupils succeed in school in Chapter 5.

Chapter 5

Assisted Reading and Dyslexia, The study "Empowering with Technology: Harnessing the Potential of Assistive Tools for Dyslexic Learners"

We'll look at how assistive technology can help dyslexic kids by changing the learning environment. Assistive technology, which includes everything from specialized software to cutting-edge apps, offers a plethora of resources that can level the playing field and empower dyslexic persons with the tools they need to overcome reading and writing issues. We can create a learning environment that accommodates dyslexia and maximizes the potential of every student by understanding the resources at our disposal and how to use them.

Learning About Dyslexia-Related Assistive Technology

Assistive technology encompasses a wide range of equipment and programs designed to aid people who are experiencing specific learning issues. These technology innovations can provide dyslexic students with personalized support tailored to their specific needs. Typical examples of dyslexic reading aid technologies include:

Text-to-voice (TTS) Programming:

TTS programming changes over composed text into spoken voice, permitting dyslexic understudies to get to text-based content. The use of innovation can lessen understanding weaknesses and work on understanding.

Speech-to-Text (STT) software allows dyslexic youngsters to dictate their ideas and thoughts, converting spoken words into written text. This tool can help with spelling problems and boost writing productivity.

There are various applications planned explicitly for dyslexic students, including intuitive activities, phonics instruction, and spelling practice. These projects can furnish understudies with a drawing-in and pleasant growth opportunity.

- **Book recordings**: For youngsters who battle to understand print, book recordings give an elective technique for getting to writing and instructive assets. Paying attention to book recordings can assist with expanding both understanding familiarity and cognizance.

- **Mind Planning Programming:** Understudies with dyslexia can all the more promptly frame expositions and plan for tests by utilizing mind planning devices to sort out their viewpoints graphically.

Learning Technology Integration

To effectively coordinate assistive innovation into the educational experience, teachers and guardians should know about each dyslexic understudy's particular requirements. Cooperative conversations can assist with choosing the proper instruments and techniques to help an individual's scholarly excursion.

Teachers might remember assistive innovation for illustration arrangements and homeroom exercises to further develop availability and cooperation. For instance, utilizing TTS programming during perusing exercises can assist with obliging dyslexic understudies and permit them to partake all the more effectively in class conversations.

 Additionally, offering dyslexic kids admittance to speech-to-text devices while allocated composing undertakings permits them to express their thoughts without being restricted by spelling difficulties.

Promoting self-determination and self-advocacy

Aside from boosting academic performance, assistive technology increases independence and self-advocacy skills in dyslexic pupils. By providing students with access to these materials, educators can empower them to take ownership of their education and enhance their problem-solving abilities.

Teachers and guardians can urge dyslexic understudies to study and explore different avenues regarding different assistive innovations so they can pick the assistive advances that best suit their learning inclinations and styles. By underlining the useful advantages of assistive innovation on scholastic achievement, dyslexic understudies can be convinced to embrace these assets enthusiastically.

Taking Care of Any Issues

Even though employing assistive technology has numerous advantages, there may be issues that arise when it is used. Among the issues are:

-Guaranteeing that every individual who needs support gets it, no matter what their monetary circumstance or mechanical necessities.

- **Overreliance**: Advancing a reasonable utilization of innovation while guaranteeing that understudies likewise partake in more customary perusing and composing exercises.

- **Continuous Preparation and Help:** Guaranteeing that understudies, educators, and guardians get progress preparation and help to utilize assistive innovation.

We can establish a dyslexia-accommodating climate that embraces the force of improvement to help learning and discerning accomplishment by eliminating these boundaries and empowering the ethical utilization of assistive turn of events.

In Chapter 6, we examine explicit strategies and approaches for pursuing and keeping in touch with dyslexic students, as we give teachers and guardians a total tool stash to help dyslexic individuals in the learning process.

Chapter 6

Reading and Writing Strategies

"Nurturing Literacy: Giving Dyslexic Learners Useful Reading and Writing Techniques"

We dive into a complete arrangement of strategies and approaches intended to help dyslexic students in their perusing and composing ventures. These proof-based techniques try to further develop understanding familiarity, phonological mindfulness, and composing abilities, permitting dyslexic people to flourish in their proficiency advancement.

Multisensory Approaches to Reading Instruction

Multisensory education is a cornerstone of effective reading support for dyslexic students. Multisensory techniques cater to varied learning styles by activating several senses—visual, aural, and kinesthetic—and reinforcing links between letters, sounds, and words. Key components of multimodal reading education include:

- Phonemic Mindfulness Exercises: Provide a range of phonological exercises that provide an emphasis on classifying, combining, and managing explicit sounds in words. Understudies can make use of tangible things like sand or beautiful lettering to increase their chances of success.

- Orton-Gillingham Approach: This systematic, sequential, and cumulative approach emphasizes phonics, decoding, and spelling standards. The Orton-Gillingham technique caters to individual learning demands and emphasizes mastery before moving on to other ideas.

Imagining and Communicating: Train youngsters to envision and articulate their thoughts as they read. This improves discernment and takes into consideration a superior perception of the substance.

Phonics, Phonological Awareness, and Fluency Strategies

Phonics teaching is essential for dyslexic students to correctly decode and encode words. Explicitly explaining the links between letters and sounds can considerably increase reading accuracy. Some ways of teaching phonics to dyslexic students include:

- **Decodable Texts**: Use texts with predictable and phonetically regular words that correspond to the phonics concepts being taught. These texts provide enough practice and reinforce newly acquired phonetic skills.

- **Word Families**: Grouping words with similar phonetic instances (such as - at, - it, - an) may aid dyslexic pupils in discovering standard spelling patterns.

- **Syllable Division Rules:** Showing syllable division rules can help disentangle multisyllabic words and increment in general understanding familiarity.

To further develop understanding familiarity, give chances to continue pursuing natural writing, and use book recordings to demonstrate familiar perusing.

Improving Writing and Composition Skills

Developing writing abilities is critical for dyslexic learners to successfully convey their thoughts and ideas. Providing explicit coaching in the writing process can help dyslexic pupils organize their thoughts and improve their written representation. Some writing development tactics include:

- **Realistic Coordinators**: Utilize visual instruments, for example, realistic coordinators to help students plan and design their composition. Coordinators, for example, mind maps or storyboards, help in the plan of consideration.

-Support the utilization of talk-to-message programming to decrease spelling challenges and let understudies focus on offering their viewpoints verbally.

Give sentence beginnings or edges to help muddle sentence structure at the beginning and to energize sentence augmentation.

- **Modifying Help**: Exhibit self-adjusting approaches and proposition useful study to students so they can work on their arrangement and foster confidence in the inventive flow.

Increasing Reading and Writing Confidence

Building perusing and composing certainty is basic for dyslexic students to embrace their specific gifts and vanquish issues. Far help certainty includes:

- **Empowering and raising analysis:** See and make up for accomplishments, paying little mind to how little.

- Little Assembling or Buddy Sponsorship: Permit dyslexic understudies the chance to collaborate in little social events or with dependable allies to assemble assurance and motivation.

- Autonomous Understanding Decision: Permit understudies to choose books of individual interest and reasonable perusing levels to increment understanding commitment and satisfaction.

Via these methodologies, educators, and watchmen can develop an environment that maintains dyslexic students' insightful gifts and energizes a durable love for examining and making.

In Chapter 7, we examine specific problems that dyslexic individuals have when studying mathematics and propose targeted techniques to promote dyscalculia and mathematical achievement.

Chapter 7:

Overcoming Obstacles and Promoting Numerical Success in Math and Dyslexia

"Motivation for Mathematical Minds: Managing Dyscalculia and Giving Dyslexic Math Learners More Control

We are going to explore the connection between dyslexia and the learning disability in math known as dyscalculia. It is essential to comprehend the difficulties dyslexic math students confront to build focused interventions that advance numerical competence and raise mathematical confidence. Dyslexic people can excel in the field of mathematics if we support cutting-edge teaching strategies and encourage a growth mindset.

The Math Learning Disorder: Understanding Dyscalculia

The capacity to understand and deal with numbers is impacted by the specific learning condition known as dyscalculia. Due to the comparable underlying cognitive issues that both dyslexia and dyscalculia share, such as problems in working memory and issues interpreting symbols and sequences, dyslexic people are more likely to acquire dyscalculia.

Typical indications of dyscalculia in dyslexic students include:

- Similarity issues with mathematical associations and ideas.
- Troubles doing basic numerical tasks (expansion, deduction, increase, and division).
- Hardships recollecting math ideas and activities.
- The powerlessness to fathom word issues and convert them into numerical techniques.

Methods for Teaching Math to Dyslexic Students

Teachers can use focused tactics that meet their specific learning needs to assist dyslexic math students. Several good strategies are as follows:

-From Matter to Extraction:
Development of mathematical cycles and thinking through the use of multimodal circumstances, including the use of manipulatives and visual peers.

- **Substance-to-Extract** Approach: To help to learn, bit by bit move from manipulatives, which are unmistakable portrayals, to images and numbers, which are dynamic ideas.

Math storyboards are visual portrayals of word issues made to help dyslexic understudies figure out the setting of the issue and separate it into successive advances.

- Mental helpers and Memory Helps: Making sense of rhymes and memory helps to assist understudies with retaining math realities and strategies.

- Building Math Jargon: Teaching understudies in math-explicit jargon and officially characterizing numerical wording.

Increasing mathematical proficiency and self-assurance

Mathematical success for dyslexic learners depends on fostering numeracy, which is the capacity to comprehend and manipulate numbers efficiently. To help dyslexic pupils develop their mathematical confidence, educators and parents can:

-**Advancing Critical thinking**: Allowing understudies the opportunity to take care of genuine issues and do numerical examinations to intrigue them and work on their numerical thinking skills.

- **Customizing Learning:** Fitting numerical preparation to meet the necessities and learning inclinations of every understudy, considering the likelihood that dyslexic understudies might require extra time and an assortment of helping techniques to comprehend numerical thoughts completely.

- **Growth mentality**: Stressing that mathematical skills can be acquired via work and practice, this strategy encourages students to see math with a growth mentality.

-**Mathematical Games and Enigmas:** Counting games and puzzles that both test and back mathematical thoughts.

Technology Use in Math Education

The improvement of math skills named dyslexic students can be significantly aided by assistive technology. Math-specific apps and interactive software, for example, can engage dyslexic kids and help them remember mathematical ideas. The benefits of math-related technologies include the following:

-Bit by bit Direction: Teaching understudies through intelligent models and nitty gritty clarifications.

-Aural assistance for mathematics questions and topics is provided through sound assistance.

-Depictions in Pictures:: Making an effort to understand things with the aid of frames and visuals.

The different numerical capacities of dyslexic students can be commended by teachers for using innovation to make a dynamic and comprehensive number-related learning climate.

By embracing dyslexic students' numerical potential, we open the entryway for them to form into confident issue solvers and numerical masterminds. Giving exhortation and help to dyslexic individuals as they take on new scholastic difficulties, Section 8 investigates the progress to secondary school and college

Chapter 8

Transitioning to High School and College

"Dyslexic Learners in Higher Education: Beyond the Horizon"

Let's talk about the particular problems and opportunities that dyslexic students have as they enter high school and college. Academic demands and increasing independence might bring new challenges, but with the correct assistance, dyslexic individuals can succeed in higher education and beyond.

Getting Through High School

For dyslexic students, the transition to high school can be both exhilarating and terrifying. The larger school setting, different classes, and more sophisticated academic demands can all pose extra obstacles. To achieve a smooth transition, instructors, parents, and students should use the following strategies:

-Self-Support Abilities: Urge dyslexic understudies to convey their necessities and look for help from educators and school staff. Creating self-backing abilities permits understudies to play a functioning job in their schooling.

- IEP or 504 Arrangement Survey: Audit and update the Individualized Instruction Plan (IEP) or 504 Arrangement to mirror the changing scholastic necessities of the great school understudy.

- Concentrate on Abilities Preparing: Concentrate on abilities courses to help dyslexic understudies in creating effective review propensities, using time productively, and association.

-Assist with a specific subject: Give additional help or direction in subjects that are trying for understudies, like troublesome math or vernaculars.

College Preparation for Dyslexic Students

College transfer is a crucial milestone for dyslexic students. College life necessitates greater independence, time management, and self-directed learning. Educators and parents can help dyslexic students prepare for this change by doing the following:

-**School Search and Determination:** Help understudies find colleges that give dyslexia support administrations, for example, mentoring, note-taking help, and assistive innovation assets.

- **School Application Interaction:** Help understudies with the application interaction, including campaigning for required facilities and submitting required documentation.

-Center around self-sponsorship while getting ready to include dyslexic understudies in conveying their requirements to teachers and local area support gatherings.

- Using time productively and Chief Working: To work on scholastic achievement, center around fortifying chief abilities to work like using time effectively and association.

College Support Services

Colleges and universities are increasingly providing complete support services for students with learning challenges. Dyslexic students can benefit from:

-Handicap Backing Focuses: These offices give different administrations, for example, scholarly guiding, assistive innovation preparing, and test facilities.

-**Focusing on happy times while getting ready**. Promotion of topic-express coaching and a focus on meetings can help to learn and offer ideas for additional assistance.

- **Note-Taking Help:** A few foundations give note-taking help through peer note-takers or recording addresses.

Embracing the College Experience

Notwithstanding its difficulties, the school offers a unique chance for development and self-revelation. Urge dyslexic understudies to follow their interests, engage in clubs and associations, and go to school on occasion.

Encourage a growth mentality by emphasizing that challenges are a natural part of the learning process. Dyslexic people can build resilience and resourcefulness via effort and determination.

Career Planning and Job Success

Planning for the progress from instruction to the gig is basic for dyslexic students. Profession administration workplaces can assist with the pursuit of employment strategies, a list of qualifications composing, and interview readiness. Moreover, dyslexic individuals can utilize their capacities, for example, inventiveness, critical thinking, and imaginative reasoning, to look for fulfilling business.

By empowering dyslexic understudies all through their secondary school and school professions, we empower them to arrive at their most prominent potential and propose their one-of-a-kind experiences to the world.

In Chapter 9, we focus on assisting dyslexic teens and adults with career planning and job success.

Chapter 9

Supporting Career Planning and Job Success for Dyslexic Individuals "Paving the Path to Success: Nurturing Dyslexic Individuals"

The crucial phase of helping dyslexic teens and adults navigate career planning and job success is covered in depth in this book. By identifying and exploiting their unique talents, encouraging self-advocacy, and creating an inclusive workplace, we can provide dyslexic people with the resources they need to flourish professionally and realize their career goals.

 Embrace career planning

When dyslexic teens and adults move from school to work, career preparation is crucial. To guide job decisions, it entails determining interests, abilities, and goals. Significant methods for helping dyslexic people with this process include the ones listed below:

Encourage adults and teenagers to research a range of employment options so they may match their choices with positions that are open to them.

-Callings that can be of help to dyslexics with unmistakable attributes like their creativity, versatility, and capacity to think basically ought to be thought of.

-Consider signing up for classes that offer open doors for commonsense mastering and expertise improvement. - Professional Preparation and Accreditations.

Mentorship and facilitated execution: Interface people with industry subject matter experts, guides, and business pioneers who could bring the choice to the table for astute exhortation.

Job Search Strategies

For persons with dyslexia, the job search process may be challenging, but with the right techniques, it may be made simpler. To help, educators, parents, and career counselors can:

PGuide gives help in developing cover letters and resumes that are accomplishment-focused and accessible to people with dyslexia.

-Arrange practice meetings and false meetings to assist competitors with acquiring certainty and prepare for normal inquiry questions.

- **Dyslexia Disclosure**: Talk to prospective employers about the pros and cons of declaring your dyslexia, comparing the advantages against the possibility of being treated differently.

support in the workplace and changes

The development of an inclusive workplace is essential for the success of dyslexic personnel. Employers may utilize the following facilities and services:

Admittance to Assistive Innovation: Make assistive innovation devices, like screen perusers or discourse-to-message programming, accessible to make perusing and composing undertakings more straightforward.

Offer remote work decisions or adaptable plans for getting work done to oblige individual requests and advance balance between fun and serious activities.

Energize the utilization of errand records and visual coordinators to organize your assignments and deal with your time successfully.

- A lovely and merciful workplace: Empower a workplace where individuals feel calm requesting help and talking about their necessities.

Developing Self-Advocacy Skills

It is crucial to teach self-advocacy skills to dyslexic adults and teenagers in both academic and professional settings. People ought to be inspired to:

Know about Their Privileges: Teach yourself about the Americans with Handicaps Act (ADA) and other relevant regulations' arrangements about the privileges of handicapped individuals in the working environment.

- **Express demands clearly:** Show them how to do this at work or in class, depending on the situation.

To support their self-assurance, urge dyslexics to be particularly themselves and to request help when they need it.

- **Recognize**. To get inspiration and direction, get in touch with capable, nearby neighborhood groups.

Taking Professional Development Seriously

People with dyslexia should be encouraged to look into chances for career growth and promotion as well as to pursue ongoing professional development. Their employment experience can be improved, and higher degrees or qualifications can lead to new opportunities.

We help dyslexic teenagers and adults reach their full potential in the workplace by offering support with career planning, job search strategies, and self-advocacy.

In Chapter 10, we concentrate on spreading awareness of dyslexia in communities and schools to foster an atmosphere of tolerance and understanding for all people.

Chapter 10:

Dyslexia Mindfulness and Making Comprehensive People Group

"Observing Variety: Bringing issues to light of Dyslexia and Making Comprehensive People group"

Allow us to stress the meaning of dyslexia mindfulness and its effect on creating comprehensive networks. By creating information, compassion, and backing for dyslexic people, we can obliterate marks of shame and urge everybody to see the value in variety and different learning styles.

Raising Dyslexia Mindfulness

Dyslexia mindfulness is the foundation for fostering a dyslexia-accommodating society. It involves teaching people, schools, organizations, and networks about dyslexia, its highlights, and the challenges that dyslexic students experience. Key endeavors to raise dyslexia mindfulness include:

- Execute dyslexia mindfulness drives in schools to instruct understudies, educators, and staff about the condition's commonness, confusion, and compelling remediation choices.

- **Parent Instruction**: Give preparation and data to guardians on identifying dyslexia, getting support, and keeping up with positive home circumstances for dyslexic students.

- **Work environment Preparing:** Hold preparing workshops for businesses and representatives to assist them with figuring out dyslexia, advance comprehensive work environment conditions, and execute fitting changes.

Sympathy and Understanding

Sympathy and understanding are basic in helping dyslexic people and empowering consideration. Compassion permits individuals to relate to the encounters and issues of dyslexic students, fabricating a thoughtful and strong climate. Key ways for expanding sympathy include:

-To expand the consciousness of the novel attributes and difficulties that accompany dyslexia, counsel dyslexics to share their encounters and triumphs.

- **Refinement Studios**: Hold sharpening studios and recreations that permit members to encounter dyslexia-related impediments, advancing compassion and appreciation for changed advancing necessities.

-While making an effort to avoid dismissing terms and stereotypes associated with dyslexia and other learning impairments, initiate the use of simple languages.

Making dyslexia-accommodating schools requires a pledge to offer full help for dyslexic understudies. A few qualities of a dyslexia-accommodating school climate include:

- **Early Intercession**: Carry out early distinguishing proof and mediation projects to recognize battling perusers when doable.

- **Individualized Help**: Make redid learning plans and alterations designated to the particular necessities of dyslexic understudies.

- **Instructor Preparing**: Give proficient advancement valuable open doors to instructors to work on their attention to dyslexia and learn fitting educating rehearses.

- **Dyslexia Asset Focuses**: Make asset focuses that proposition particular materials, assistive innovation, and instructive apparatuses to dyslexic understudies.

Bringing Dyslexia Mindfulness Up in Networks

Dyslexia mindfulness ought to grow past schools and work environments to the whole local area. Underlining the significance of changed learning styles can foster comprehensive mentalities and acknowledgment. Among the techniques for expanding dyslexia mindfulness in networks are:

- Local area Occasions: Hold dyslexia mindfulness occasions, studios, and classes in public venues, libraries, and other nearby scenes.

-Make associations with encompassing affiliations, support gatherings, and associations to build attention to dyslexia and subsidize drivers.

To dissipate fantasies and predispositions of dyslexia, energize precise and positive depictions in the media.

Embracing Inclusivity: Moving Past Dyslexia

While dyslexia mindfulness is significant, supporting inclusivity reaches out past dyslexia to all people with different learning styles and needs. Embracing neurodiversity and supporting comprehensive instructive and proficient conditions benefits everybody since it praises extraordinary capacities and adds to an understanding and caring society.

We give the preparation to a general public where dyslexic people might flourish, variety is commended, and all students can understand their maximum capacity through raising dyslexia mindfulness and building comprehensive networks.

Congrats! You have arrived at the finish of this dyslexia book. This thorough handbook endeavors to raise information, understanding, and backing for dyslexic individuals, empowering them to embrace their special characteristics and make progress in all pieces of life. Recollecting that raising dyslexia mindfulness and inclusivity is a continuous interaction and that by cooperating, we can make a more splendid and more comprehensive future for everybody.

Chapter 11

Looking Ahead: Developments in Dyslexia Research and Support

Here, my focus is on highlighting the most recent developments in dyslexia research and the changing nature of the dyslexia assistance sector. We look forward to exciting advances that will change how we approach dyslexia awareness and intervention as technology, educational practices, and scientific understanding advance. These developments will further empower dyslexic people.

Dyslexia Research Advancements

The understanding of the neural mechanisms behind dyslexia has been greatly aided by developments in neuroscience and cognitive psychology. We are learning more about how the brain processes information and how that affects reading and language abilities as research investigations continue to shed light on the neural foundation of dyslexia.

The development of brain imaging methods like functional MRI (fMRI) has allowed researchers to monitor brain activity while people read in real time. These investigations have shown that there are differences in the brain activation patterns of dyslexic and non-dyslexic people, which is important information for developing focused therapies.

Finding particular genes linked to gene-dyslexia susceptibility has advanced significantly in genetic research. Understanding the genetic causes of dyslexia can help with early detection and customized treatment plans depending on a person's genetic profile.

Assistive tools and technology

Modern assistive aids and learning materials for people with dyslexia are made possible thanks to technological advancements. A multitude of dynamic and interesting tools are now available to dyslexic learners because of the ongoing development of user-friendly apps, software, and internet platforms.

Man-made brainpower (simulated intelligence) has immense potential for tending to dyslexia and is as of now changing how training is given. To give individualized data and suggestions to dyslexic understudies, man-made intelligence-fueled learning stages can look at explicit learning inclinations and styles.

Because of their exhibition information, AI calculations can expect youngsters to understand difficulties and suggest explicit medicines. As simulated intelligence is created, it might turn out to be more pivotal for arranging early dyslexia screening and intercessions.

Perusing and composing guidance might be improved by using expanded reality (AR) and computer-generated reality (VR) in instructive conditions. Multimodal learning conditions that take special care of different learning inclinations can be created using these vivid exercises.

By checking and controlling their feelings of anxiety during learning exercises, wearable innovation, and biofeedback strategies might assist dyslexic understudies with succeeding scholastically.

Changing Your Mindset to Accept Neurodiversity

A progressive movement toward integrating neurodiversity in learning environments and workplaces is occurring as knowledge of dyslexia rises. Supporters of neurodiversity contend that rather than being seen as deficiencies, dyslexia, and other learning differences should be seen as variations in how the human brain functions.

This mentality change promotes the celebration of varied thinking approaches and cultivates inclusive workplaces that cater to various learning requirements. A more upbeat and inspiring narrative about dyslexia might be encouraged by focusing on strengths and potential rather than restrictions.

Initiatives and Policy Shifts Around the World

Global initiatives to support dyslexic people in education and careers have been prompted by growing dyslexia awareness. To more effectively incorporate support and adjustments for dyslexia, many nations are altering their educational policies and curricular frameworks.

With businesses appreciating the benefits of varied talent and establishing inclusive hiring procedures and work cultures, initiatives to promote dyslexia-friendly workplaces are increasingly gaining traction.

As we move into the future, we anticipate substantial advancements in dyslexia research, technology, and teaching. By embracing these advancements and keeping our dedication to dyslexia awareness and inclusivity, we can keep building a world where people with dyslexia may prosper and contribute their unique perspectives to society. By cooperating, we can make everyone's future inclusive and promising.

Chapter 12

Dyslexia Promotion and Having a Drawn-out Effect

We should investigate the pertinence of dyslexia promotion and the jobs of people, networks, and associations in significantly impacting dyslexic individuals. We can make a fairer and stronger world for everybody by cooperating to bring issues to light, advocate for positive change, and embrace dyslexia-comprehensive practices.

The Promotion Impact

Dyslexia promotion is basic in creating great change and engaging dyslexic people. Advocates try to raise dyslexia mindfulness, disperse fantasies, and entryway for strategy changes that improve admittance to assets and backing.

People and families affected by dyslexia can become advocates by sharing their accounts, partaking in mindfulness drives, and associating with instructive and official accomplices. Dyslexic individuals can be areas of strength for me, by filling in as good examples and rousing others to embrace their capacities and potential.

Comprehensive Training for Dyslexia

Backing drives are basic in advancing dyslexia-comprehensive schooling at all levels. To more readily serve dyslexic students, schools and instructive foundations can utilize proof-based techniques, give educators preparing for dyslexia support, and foster committed asset places.

Backers can work with instructors, educational committees, and policymakers to campaign for early dyslexia screening, brief meditations, and the execution of Individualized Training Plans (IEPs) or 504 Designs to guarantee custom-made help for dyslexic children.

Corporate and Working Environment Promotion

Pushing for dyslexia-comprehensive arrangements in the work environment is basic for encouraging societies that advance variety and oblige different learning styles. Corporate support could incorporate pushing for the accessibility of assistive innovation, adaptable work courses of action, and dyslexia mindfulness preparation for staff.

Organizations can effectively draw in and support dyslexic ability by perceiving the exceptional perspectives and critical thinking gifts that dyslexic people deal with in the business.

Joint effort Organizations

To have a drawn-out influence, dyslexia gatherings, instructors, legislators, partnerships, and networks should cooperate. Cooperating, partners might pool assets, share best practices, and expand the range of dyslexia mindfulness and backing exercises.

Joint effort can likewise bring about the arrangement of dyslexia teams or working gatherings devoted to tending to dyslexia-related troubles and introducing novel arrangements.

Using Media and Innovation

The effect of media and innovation on open insight couldn't possibly be more significant. Supporters can utilize online entertainment stages, sites, and conventional word sources to get out the right data about dyslexia, feature examples of overcoming adversity, and fight shame.

Support endeavors can utilize virtual and increased reality encounters to encourage sympathy and understanding, permitting people to encounter dyslexia-related issues straightforwardly.

Partaking in Science and Exploration

Supporting dyslexia research is basic to encouraging comprehension. We might interpret the problem and make successful intercessions. Gathering pledges for research drives, supporting dyslexia research foundations, and connecting with researchers and specialists to overcome any barrier between information and practice are instances of promotion activities.

Worldwide Dyslexia Promotion

Dyslexia promotion is a worldwide development, and cross-line joint effort is basic. Promoters can help unfamiliar dyslexia associations, partake in diverse ventures, and offer viable backing strategies to construct a worldwide work to propel dyslexia information and help.

In Chapter 12, we comprehend the changing force of dyslexia support and its true capacity for long-haul impact. By embracing dyslexia-comprehensive methodologies in training, working environments, and networks, we establish a climate wherein dyslexic people can prosper, contribute, and arrive at their maximum capacity. Dyslexia promotion is a continuous excursion, and together, we can make a more promising time to come that commends variety and enables everybody, no matter what their one-of-a-kind learning techniques.

Due to their setting explicit implications, the accompanying key expressions are utilized throughout the book:

1. **Dyslexia**: Dyslexia is a particular learning issue that brings on some issues with perusing, spelling, and composing despite typical knowledge and respectable training.

2. **Prevalence**: The extent of a populace that has a condition or confusion, like dyslexia, out of nowhere.

3. Unmistakable attributes of dyslexia, like troubles with perusing, translating, and phonological handling.

4. **Intervention**: Moves or projects made to help and support dyslexic individuals in working on their composition and understanding abilities.

5. Multisensory: Integrating visual, aural, and sensation faculties to further develop learning and perception.

6. Phonological mindfulness is the capacity to recognize and manage the different sounds that contain words. It is an essential expertise for perusing and spelling.

7. Changes to the learning climate to more readily oblige dyslexic students and work on their admittance to information.

8. Assistive innovation is gear or programming intended to assist dyslexic individuals with beating, perusing, and composing troubles. Text-to-discourse and discourse-to-message applications are instances of such apparatuses.

9. Inclusive: To esteem variety and guarantee that all individuals, incorporating those with dyslexia, have equivalent admittance to open doors.

10. Numeracy: For dyslexic numerical understudies, the capacity to handle and work with numbers is basic.

11. Vocation arranging is the most common way of choosing an expert course founded on interests, capacities, and objectives.

12. Self-Advocacy: A dyslexic individual's ability to communicate their requirements, look for help, and protect themselves in scholar and expert settings.

13. **Empathy**: The capacity to fathom and discuss the thoughts and considerations of people who are dyslexic, while likewise giving a caring and steady climate.

14. **Neurodiversity**: The acknowledgment and pleasure in the changed manners by which individuals' minds and perspectives capability, is dyslexic to incorporate the people who.

15. **Worldwide Backing:** Endeavors to advance receptiveness and resistance all over the planet by expanding information and backing for dyslexia on a worldwide scale.

Understanding this language and its definitions is fundamental for getting a handle on the setting of the book's points on dyslexia, mindfulness, backing, and strengthening.